GioBatta Bear

GB Bear and the pilot's license

Deborah Faenza and Gianni Riccardi

GB Bear and the pilot's license

www.gbbear.com

Translation: Gina Copeland

Written and illustrated by Gianni Riccardi and Deborah Faenza

To Veronica and Alessandro: Thank you for inspiring us."

In the Italian Riviera, a cute little bear with an all-blue fur coat lives in a very small town along the sea. His name is GioBatta, but everyone calls him GB. GB likes to start his day by eating a delicious breakfast.

From his home's terrace you can see the sea and seagulls are happily fluttering all around. Every morning, his buddy Riccardo, known as Ricky, stops by to say hello.

"Ciao GB", happily waved Ricky, "I was riding my bike and came by to say hi!".

"Ciao Ricky, would you like a piece of toast with pesto on it?".

"Why don't you eat toast and jelly for breakfast, like everyone else?" Ricky curiously asked.

"You know why! This pesto is way too good!", replied GB, as he slurped a spoonful of the runny green sauce.

In that exact moment, the rumbling of an airplane caught their attention.

"Look...a white trail from a plane!" GB pointed, widening his eyes.

"I have decided. I want to be a pilot too!".

"It' s very hard to become a pilot", Ricky said in his teacherly voice.

"I don't care! I can do it!", GB resolutely replied, "I'm done with my pesto toast. Let's go look at the flying school!".

The two buddies hopped into GB's red scooter-truck (Ape) and happily headed straight to the flying school.

The flying school was very busy with aircraft constantly flying up and down from the sky.

"Look, how cool that red plane is? Let's go ask them for a ride", GB hopefully exclaimed.

"B-But, but, wait. They must be very busy", stammered Ricky.

"Sir?", asked GB, "Would you please take us on a short plane ride?".

The flight Instructor glanced at GB and then answered, "I'm the Chief Flight Instructor. If you want to try and pilot a plane, wait for me over there and wear this yellow vest. I will put fuel in the airplane and then I will come to pick you up".

The instructor handed headsets to GB and Ricky and then helped them board the plane.

"Wow! This is great! He's taking us in the air and will let me fly the plane", exclaimed GB.

"But I am s-s-scared", complained Ricky.

"Come on, don't be afraid! We are going to have fun", said GB.

"I am all set. When are we taking off?", GB asked impatiently as he hopped on the wing.

"Ricky, you take the back seat and put on the headset", said the instructor.

"GB, you sit in front next to me. That is the student pilot's seat. Make sure that you do exactly what I say and don't touch anything unless I instruct you to do so. Got it?"

"Yes sir. I got it", GB confirmed, with a big smile on his face.

"Let's hope so", whispered Ricky to himself.

The plane took off into a strong headwind and went toward the sea. Immediately, the instructor said, "GB, rotate the yoke to the left and pull it gently toward you, so that the plane will not descend".

"Following your orders, sir! This is wonderful", declared GB.

"Ricky,

how are you doing?".

"N–n–not so good.

When are we going to l–l–land?".

"Come on Ricky, just relax and enjoy the flight", said GB. "Check this out.

I will turn on the air conditioning to help you feel better".

Without even finishing the sentence, GB had already hit the switch.

"Noooooo, that's not the air conditioning!", exclaimed the instructor in astonishment.

GB had turned off the engine instead of turning on the air conditioning.

"I told you not to touch anything without asking first". The instructor scolded him, saying "Now we have to turn the engine on again with the emergency procedure".

BEEP BEEP BEEP

"I am so sorry, teacher", explained GB. "I thought I could make it cooler for Ricky!".

"For all the c-c-carrots in the world, let's hope the engine will s-s-start again", shouted worried Ricky as he flew out his seat.

The instructor read the emergency check-list and followed all the required steps to turn the engine back on and flew them back to the airstrip.

"That was amazing!" GB excitedly exclaimed after they landed.

"Land, sweet land!", exclaimed Ricky.

"Now I KNOW, I want to get my pilot's license", proclaimed GB while Ricky was still lying down kissing the ground.

"Uh, are you sure? After what we just went through?", asked Ricky.

"What are you talking about, Ricky?

Didn't you see how well I flew?", replied GB.

"Yes, but you had the instructor on board", pointed out Ricky worriedly.

"You worry too much! I have made up my mind Ricky", said GB.

"I will get my pilot's license! Then we both fly to Argentina and bring some pesto to my cousin Luciano. He will be so happy to see us! I am sure he will throw us a party!".

Right away, GB started studying to become a pilot, but he found out it was more difficult than he thought. "You were right, Ricky", he admitted. "It is hard work. I have to study a lot".

Ricky remembered what GB said before and made fun of him, saying "I've made up my mind. I'm taking pesto to Argentina!".

"You will see. I WILL make it. I'm sure of it", GB reassured him.

GB worked very hard. He studied and often practiced flying with the instructor. Finally, he was able to take his first solo flight.

"Wow, you did it!", shouted Ricky to his friend as GB parked the plane.

"It was fantastic, Ricky!", said GB. "There were all sorts of little clouds and lots of seagulls flying in the air next to me".

The instructor proudly complimented GB, "You did really well. Now that you are a pilot, we can celebrate you. I will now pin the eagle on your chest. It is the symbol of every pilot. Be very proud of it".

"Ricky, Ricky! Look at me, I'm a true pilot!", declared GB.

"Now we can fly to Argentina to visit my cousin Luciano and bring him pesto. Are you ready?".

"Hehe, I knew it", said Ricky. "We have not even celebrated your success and you are ready for a new adventure".

"You can say that loud and clear my friend", replied GB. "But, first, would you like to celebrate with some pesto flavoured ice-cream?".

"For all the carrots, of course I do! But for me, I choose carrot flavour!".

So, where do you think the next story will bring GioBatta and Ricky to? Be sure to follow them in the their next adventure.

"THE ITALIAN RIVIERA" is in Europe, where Italy is by the Mediterranean Sea. It is famous for the clear sea, the romantic fisherman's villages and the flowers.

"CIAO" means hello in Italian and It is pronounced "chow".

"PESTO" is an Italian sauce. It is made from the best basil grown only in areas close to the city of Genova.

"APE" is a three-wheel scooter-truck very popular in Italy for its small dimensions. It is often driven by farmers in medieval villages with narrow roads between the houses, but It became also very popular upon teen agers in its particular version "CROSS".

"GELATO" means ice-cream in Italian. The tipical creamy one is made out of fresh fruit and blanded whole ingredients, without artificial colours or flavours. Often the kids add whipped cream on top of their cone.

Printed by Amazon Italia Logistica S.r.l.
Torrazza Piemonte (TO), Italy

51165920R00020